# TECHNICAL
# MINDS

*Leading and Getting the Best Work
from Your Technically-Minded Team*

# Ara W. Nazarian

ISBN: 145158315X
ISBN-13: 9781451583151
Library of Congress Control Number: 2010905294

To my daughters with love,
Christine and Rita

# Acknowledgments:

I want to thank Frederik Nanoo Staal
and Marc Nussbaum for their tremendous
contributions and support for this book.

# Table of Contents

# Preface

Here's the good news: Congratulations! You've been promoted!

The bad news is: Who is going to coach you to be a good leader?

You are brilliant in your field of technology, so much so that your organization has put you in charge of other employees—techies and perhaps non-techies too. Now what?

If you're like most technologically oriented people, you have never been given any specific training in the art and science of leading people. And now that your boss has promoted you to a management position—or a higher management position—wouldn't it be great if somebody handed you a manual that would tell you exactly what to do in every aspect of your new role as a leader?

Well, here's more good news, and there's no bad news to follow: You are holding that manual in your hands.

This book was born of my own experience as an engineer and as a leader at a few very successful (and a few not-so-successful) companies I worked for.

Unfortunately, all the respect we enjoyed and our technological genius did not suddenly transform into managerial greatness at the click of a mouse or the touch of a magic wand.

With this book I intend to equip you with the tools you need to be a truly outstanding leader. You wouldn't have been promoted if you had lacked the technical skills necessary to excel in your field. But managerial and leadership skills are something entirely different. Together, we'll discover what it takes to be a great leader in technology-based organizations.

Just now I used the words art and science to describe what management is, because it is really a little bit of both. People are not data. They do not take kindly to impersonal commands. People cannot be "batched," let alone folded, spindled, or mutilated. And techies also present their own unique set of issues when being managed. While they may be able to create phenomenal results with a keyboard and mouse pad, they may be less comfortable with the kind of one-to-one interaction or presentation skills that managers require.

So this is your opportunity to learn how to get the best work from the people who now report to you. The situation is often complicated by the fact that you may have been their coworker yesterday, and today you are their boss. When that transition happens, it can be awkward for everyone concerned. Perhaps there was someone in your department who thought that he or she was better qualified to manage and lead than you. How do you handle that delicate situation? Or perhaps there is someone whose work habits are interfering with your department's productivity instead of contributing to it. That's not so great, either. Your mission as a leader is to ensure that you've got the right people doing the right jobs in the best possible way, so as to maximize their contribution to your department and to your organization and to help them realize their own career goals.

In my own personal experience as an engineering manager, I've faced just about every difficult situation a boss can encounter. I'm here to share my experience—often painfully gained—with you now.

I invite you to join me, then, on a journey that will help you find new levels of excellence that will offer you the kind of job satisfaction and career experience that you can find only when you become responsible for a group of brilliant, driven, and sometimes cranky or even obstinate individuals who fall under the broad rubric of techies.

# Introduction

The inspiration for this book came from a conversation with an old friend. One day he said to me, "Ara, since you've been unofficially assigned by the company to mentor many of our managers and directors, why don't you write a book that captures your experiences and can be used by others to give them a head start?"

After thinking about this for a while, I decided he was onto something. So I sat down to write a book that I could personally use to simplify my job of training new or aspiring managers inside high-tech organizations. The idea was to produce a sort of "leadership requirements" document that I could hand to someone as a starting point. I would then act as a mentor to help him or her put these leadership principles into practice within both their own teams and the larger organization.

While there is obviously no substitute for experience, preparation can go a long way. My intent in this book is to help scientists and engineers become better leaders by preparing them to internalize and use leadership principles with confidence. I will also illustrate how to put these principles to work within your own organization. My goal is also to help managers get into the fast lane on the leadership ladder.

This work distills thirty years of observing and training leaders in various organizational businesses including successful startups, failed startups, and large multinational companies in their high-growth, mature, and contracting stages. The intent is to identify the skills and values of strong leaders and transfer this knowledge to the reader using real-life examples.

I have coached many employees throughout my career and I've enjoyed watching them grow and succeed. In the pages that you are about to read, I'll share my leadership principles and key concepts through actual situations. Sometimes my observations illustrate what works, and sometimes they illustrate—often very clearly—what *doesn't* work.

It is important to acknowledge and credit others whenever possible (more about this as a leadership principle later), so, to be clear, I didn't come up with all these wonderful ideas myself. Some of the key concepts in this book come from reading other books over the years; others I have picked up at lectures; and many ideas come from the people I've worked with. But I have personally tested and practiced each of these key concepts day-to-day as a manager and leadership mentor in several engineering corporations.

Throughout my career I've made it a point to preserve what works, prune what does not work, and continually improve the clarity of my values as a leader. Eventually, I was able to condense the key elements of my experience into ten chapters. These ideas have been developed and refined inside some of America's most successful high-technology companies. Having personally practiced and taught them to my managers and directors, I can attest to their effectiveness.

In this book, a *manager* is defined as a person who manages people regardless of his or her level or title in the organization. For example: the word *manager* can refer to a person who is a VP or vice president.

If you are managing people in a technology company or aspiring to be more effective in your current position, this book will help you. It is my desire that my experiences may serve to reinforce your own personal goals for continuous improvement. If you are tasked with mentoring and developing managers or directors of your own, I hope this book will provide many years of service as one you can feel comfortable handing to your aspiring and new leaders. It's my hope that this book will spur them—and you—toward unprecedented success.

# CHAPTER 1

# Inspire and Energize

We can never underestimate the importance of energy and inspiration. These intangibles fuel the soul and keep the brain ticking.

People get inspired in different ways and for different reasons. Some people find the energy and inspiration to move forward naturally, while others need to be encouraged to start a task or undertake a mission. Energizing people is one of the oldest mechanisms leaders use to ignite the spirit of their fellow men and women as they work together to achieve their goals. I can imagine that even the caveman needed to energize his fellow cavemen to go and hunt for food. He would have reminded them how hungry they were and how delicious the meat would taste when the hunt was over!

Leaders energize their team members to get the juices flowing and keep them excited about what they are doing. In general, people get motivated to contribute to a project when they understand it and believe in it. This knowledge elevates the importance of their work beyond their basic need to have a job. This is why leaders must explain the connection between the project, the financial success of the organization, and the greater good of the company. Even more importantly, the leader needs to make people feel a connection between their work and the success of mankind as a whole. People look to a leader literally to create a vision of a bright future.

*Flashback: Mr. Zinger, a manager at a prominent high-tech company, constantly wrote demotivating or "zinger" emails to his team. It didn't matter if he was writing the email to another manager, an individual contributor, or—even worse—to a large distribution list; all of his requests for help started with an insult, followed by a demand for the person to respond or correct the situation.*

*When people got his emails, they were turned off before even understanding the existing issue. Obviously, the recipient would not get energized to resolve the issue, even if the issue was serious.*

*Other than his "zinger email" behavior, this manager was very technically savvy and understood the business very well. As a matter of fact, people respected his capabilities—but they resented his emails.*

*This manager worked for me. I discussed his behavior by first asking him, "Do you think you could have written this email in a different way, a way that actually motivated the person receiving it to help you?"*

2

The point I would like to make here is that a leader must always find a way to communicate with his or her workers in an energizing and motivating manner, regardless of where he believes the fault or problem to lie. Remember, the goal is to resolve the problem in an expeditious manner, and it must start with energizing statements.

*Mr. Zinger's emails would typically begin like so: "This is a lame answer! Ridiculous! I'm tired of this issue and your inability to resolve it. Fix this fast."*

*He could have disseminated the same information but energized the person instead, simply by saying, "I need your help. This issue has been open for a while, and you are the best person to fix it. I would really appreciate your attention. Please put in extra effort to resolve this. Thank you."*

Leaders must never demotivate their teams, no matter the circumstances.

At the other end of the spectrum, injecting positive energy into an organization breeds optimism. A leader who is walking around with positive energy is an optimism multiplier!

*Flashback: One of the VPs I worked for, Mr.Energizer, had a strong energizing effect. Whether you talked to him individually or heard him speak at a meeting, he always knew how to spark enthusiasm. After his all-hands meetings, everyone inevitably went back to work feeling motivated. Every one of his messages and emails started with something positive about accomplishments that individuals (or the team) had achieved. In this way, he communicated his message by creating a connection between the team's tasks and the goals of the organization as a whole.*

It is important to show a concrete relationship between a person's contribution and the big picture. This is a very difficult task; I have not met many leaders who are able to make this connection clearly. For example, how does one individual's effort to complete her task (say, writing a software module) relate to helping a company that claims $1 billion a year in revenue? It is the manager's job to find this relationship and explain it to his or her team. The CEO is often too far removed to explain this relationship, which makes it the first-level manager's job and no one else's.

Most corporations fail to understand that first-level managers are the most important management layer in making a company successful. They are the ones who have the primary contact with the people who are doing the actual work. After all, the high-energy, intelligent, individual contributors are the true heroes of any successful company.

More often than not, I see first-level managers who are lacking in some very basic management skills. I've seen projects and plans fail because of these managers' lack of training or mentoring skills. Corporations must pay close attention to the selection and development of first-level managers. I often see situations where the executives, VPs, and directors get more coaching and training than the first-level managers—exactly the opposite of the way it should be. If the first-level manager is not energized, how is he going to energize his team?

Energizing the team makes a huge difference in the outcome of a project. Note that energizing a team is not just giving pep talks that last a few hours, and it's not the same as a "shot in the arm." High energy and enthusiasm must permeate the culture of an organization. In other words, it must become a way of life. This energy can be built by consistently having managers behave in a fair and motivating manner. To do this, every manager from the top of the command chain to the bottom must conduct all written and verbal communication in an energizing spirit.

*Flashback: Ms. Silent, a first-level manager, never communicated her issues directly to her boss. When things went wrong, she blamed her boss for not intervening earlier when she needed help. Her resentment continued to grow when in reality it was her own failure to communicate that put her in that position.*

*Ms. Silent didn't believe it was her role to energize the troops. Her survival mechanism was to polarize her group against her boss. Over time, the entire team began to dislike the big boss and negative energy began to creep throughout the organization.*

*As the situation worsened, the group's performance grew increasingly poor. Ms. Silent managed to*

***demotivate many individual contributors by denigrating the big boss.***

This is an example of a first-level manager who killed the productivity of many individual contributors, eventually leading to issues with retention of good people. The manager failed to understand that energizing her own team was one of the key elements of her job.

No matter what is going on at the upper levels of the management chain, each manager must look in the mirror and take responsibility for making sure his or her team is energized. It's amazing how many times I've had managers (at all levels, unfortunately) come to me and say that their team is de-motivated, and that the CEO or some big VP needs to come and pump them up. Basically, they always point to some mythical person who they believe is responsible for energizing their teams. Wrong!

In these situations, it is the manager's job to motivate his or her own team. I'm not advocating that the first-level manager hide looming company-wide issues that need to be addressed by a VP or CEO. But it is the manager's job to communicate the issues in a positive light and explain how the VPs are handling the situation.

All managers at all levels are responsible for their team's motivation level. When a team is demotivated for any reason, the manager immediately responsible for the team is the first person to question. That means that if one of my direct reports is not energized, I don't even have to know the reason to be able to identify the culprit: me!

*Flashback: Early in my career, I was fortunate to inherit a highly technical group that was naturally energized and self-motivated. They were energized by the technology they were working on and the huge opportunities in revenue it represented.*

*The opportunities went beyond just making money. My group was motivated by the way their projects would change the way of life for millions of people around the world. This was an ideal place to work—the energy was high and politics were practically nonexistent.*

Unfortunately, the "tech" world does not offer these opportunities very often. That's why I highly recommend that people seek out companies or organizations that are energized with self-motivated people. Note that successful organizations are inherently energized *and* motivated. I'll repeat this: successful organizations are inherently energized and motivated. If you think these sorts of companies don't exist, think again. Many startup companies, and even some larger ones, have this type of environment.

Often startups are more productive and efficient than mature companies. They're usually energized and focused and, unlike older companies, haven't been infected with the plague of large-organization mediocrity. Large companies *can* inoculate themselves against this plague—by hiring only motivated and high-energy people and continuing to feed them with exciting projects they can connect with. However, if the first-level managers are not trained well, eventually some sub-performers will be hired.

Oftentimes, managers are pressured to hire fast. Given the lack of high-quality resources generally available, they drop the quality bar for hiring. That's when the plague starts. Highly energized organizations like start-ups don't stay energized unless the leaders of the company understand the importance of this element to their overall success. In the long term, it is better to spend extra time up front to hire people that are energized about what they are doing. A good leader recognizes the power of an energized environment and makes sure the individuals who don't fit don't get hired in the first place; if they do, they should be asked to leave.

I highly recommend that leaders walk around the organization and meet one-on-one with colleagues, peers, and subordinates. They should talk to them in meetings, in labs, and in coffee-break rooms, always sharing energy with everyone they meet—and sharing energy is always infectious. Some people think it's an inherent gift or personality trait of some gifted leaders. That's absolutely not true! It is a learned behavior, and people can learn this skill by focusing on and pronouncing the positives of every situation.

Optimism multiplies and grows like wildfire, especially if the leader and her generals encourage optimism throughout the organization. Some leaders energize so well that you can feel their positive presence as soon as they enter a room. This type of energy is not created overnight. It gets built up day after day through consistent behavior from the leader. After a while it becomes so natural to behave in this manner that people assume it's the leader's natural behavior!

One way leaders energize organizations is by recognizing the accomplishments of individuals or sub-teams in team meetings or emails every chance they get. Good leaders never take credit for themselves; instead, they recognize their people. If they can't justify giving the credit to an individual, they credit the whole team or the whole company.

The strongest motivator for technologists is being allowed and encouraged to work on different things. Many technologists lose interest when they work on one thing for a long time and the job becomes repetitive. Managers need to allow people to work on different aspects of the design or product. The good news for managers is that engineers naturally know what other areas they would like to work on and they usually request them. The bad news is finding new people or rotating existing employees into these areas. Regardless of the pain level for managers, allowing people to move around should be encouraged.

When I first started contemplating the move from hands-on technical work to management, I had to think very hard about whether or not I would enjoy this type of position. Many technical people feel that management is an overhead, superfluous, position and are not sure if managers are actually useful to the organization. I was lucky enough to have good role models who inspired me; I was very motivated by other leaders who possessed an energizing style. I saw them as people with the capacity to energize their teams and focus the work to achieve big goals. That's when I made the decision that I would either be like Mr. Energizer, or not be a manager at all.

In truth, it was the talent of one man—my role model manager—that compelled me to become a manager in the first place. His chief trait as a leader was that he had a strong presence and people wanted to emulate his style. As I look back and analyze what made him so successful, I realize that it was his energy or his aura of success, coupled with the respect he engendered, that inspired others to follow him.

The bottom line: all leaders must be energized. This behavior inspires confidence throughout the organization and helps people overcome any obstacles that may arise.

In the next chapter, we'll discuss how being optimistic is only one side of the coin. The other side is to be honest about the brutal reality of every situation.

C H A P T E R    2

# Surface and Face the "Brutal Reality"

Leaders have to understand the importance of facing reality. Although it can sometimes be painful, looking reality right in the eye is the only way to make progress. Hiding one's head in the sand is fine—for ostriches! Leaders, however, must remain vigilant and face the truth.

An unwillingness to face reality can become a manager's biggest weakness. By doing nothing while hoping problems will go away (or magically improve on their own), a manager is clinging to delusion. Many people who refuse to face real issues create their own pseudo-reality, but strong leaders have a knack for surfacing, exposing, the brutal reality of situations, and then facing that reality head-on.

Not dealing with issues early on usually just delays the inevitable. These issues always reveal themselves eventually, and they tend to surface as more ugly and painful than they were before—which means they're more costly to fix. Most people choose the path of least resistance and do nothing. It takes a lot of courage and maturity to take the road less traveled and face the issues head on.

Since most problems are addressed with some sort of change in mind, you can expect resistance from the rest of the team as you try to fix things. I've seen people fight against change that even they recognize as being necessary for the greater good. In these situations, a strong leader will not just create new rules and walk away. He or she will go face-to-face with all the detractors and discuss the solution with each of them until each and every soldier is on the winning side.

*Flashback: I remember introducing a new development tool that would bring more productivity to the team. This tool was statistically and quantitatively proven by other companies. About 20 percent of this group didn't support the change, claiming that it was a waste of time. They said the tools they were currently using were good enough.*

*After putting in my best effort to discuss this in open forums and training sessions, I still had people who were not on board. Some leaders would have just moved on with their plan, being satisfied to have at least an 80 percent buy-in. But I knew the remaining 20 percent could end up causing much bigger problems down the line. The dissenters would be prone to talk about it in the hallways and keep bringing up reasons why we shouldn't be using this new tool.*

*The brutal reality of my situation was that not everyone was on board. So, the best thing to do was to talk to every person who was not on board, one at a time, understand their viewpoint, and then find a way to bridge it.*

*As it turned out, all I had to do to get the remaining group members to accept the new system was simply talk to them and accommodate their needs by tweaking the tool. Basically, we modified the format very slightly to make these few people happy. As a result, we got all of them to buy in to the new methodology, enabling us to sail into greater productivity as a cohesive team.*

Unfortunately, this kind of success may more often be the exception than the rule. Reality says that it's impossible to have everyone on board 100 percent of the time. In the event that you can't get every member of your team to agree, you still have to forge ahead.

However, not talking about a troublesome issue is not productive and sends the wrong message to the team. By confronting the issue, your team members will understand that if there is a problem, it will be addressed and brought to an understanding or conclusion. And I say bring it to an "understanding" because you cannot always bring every issue to a conclusion that the whole team agrees on.

The manager must explain to the team, sincerely and positively, that everyone's concerns and opinions will be addressed and considered, but that the final decision will be his and his alone. He should always show respect for team members as he explains that the decision will be made for the good of the group. In these cases, a leader can benefit from discussing the issue in a forum-type setting and clarifying the long-term plan that will be implemented to address it. He should also communicate to the team that the issue may not be resolved immediately—that's generally a part of the brutal reality the organization must face.

After the initial communication with the troops, the manager should follow up periodically to show proof of progress; otherwise more anxiety and uncertainty may linger.

Here is one example of how to deal head-on with an issue that a less skilled manager may choose to ignore.

*Flashback: At the company where I worked, there was one department that was absolutely terrible about documenting their designs. Since my group was responsible for taking these designs and integrating them into a bigger system, we definitely needed the documentation improved so that we could do our job effectively. But the reality was that this group was not going to drop everything and start documenting their designs just because we asked them to.*

*So, we called a meeting with the head of the department and discussed the impact we felt from the lack of documentation. We didn't let go of the issue until we mutually agreed on a long-term plan to correct the situation—without impacting the immediate projects.*

*Then we called a meeting with my department and explained the brutal reality: there was, in fact, no documentation immediately available. However, although we would need to continue the current project without the full documentation we desired, we were happy to report that we had reached an agreement to deliver better documentation in the future.*

*Together, we explained why this issue could not be fixed instantly and assured everyone that we were committed to fixing the issue by taking "baby steps." We outlined a specific timeline for our goals and reviewed which products would have what level of documentation. In this way, we faced the reality head-on, clearing the immediate anxiety. We acknowledged the problem by implementing a plan to move forward and enact positive change.*

Leaders instinctively know that bringing issues to the surface is painful, but it often requires real-world experience to learn that discussing and dealing with issues is far more productive than not doing anything. Most managers who avoid the reality of key issues act as they do because they don't have an immediate solution. But it is still infinitely better to bring up reality— even if you have no clue how to solve the problem. This shows that, as a leader, you know what is going on, and that even if you don't have the solution, you still want to address the problem. Good leaders bring up the brutal reality and show that it can be resolved incrementally by taking small steps.

*Flashback: Once, while working in a startup company, we didn't know if we could meet next week's payroll. In the midst of these dire straits, the CEO was agonizing over whether or not to bring this brutal reality to the team and tell everyone what was going on. I was a proponent of telling the troops exactly where we were—I thought it was best that the employees make their own decision as to whether, given the problem, they wanted to stay or go.*

*While the CEO was working on some plans to bring money in, his plans weren't guaranteed. The problem was, he wasn't sure if it was wise to tell the team the truth and risk losing people and productivity, or if he should wait until the last possible moment.*

*In this case, the CEO chose the latter option. He didn't tell the troops about the lack of money because he was trying to avoid creating a panic. This might be a reasonable approach—if one can guarantee that the money will be there in time for the next payroll! As it so happened, we failed to meet payroll the following week. The team was angry at the CEO for not letting them know earlier, and as a result, they lost trust in his abilities as a leader.*

*That loss of trust was irrecoverable—and fatal. If only the CEO had surfaced the brutal reality, people would have felt like they were part of the team.*

One must always look in the mirror when things are not going well. Facing the brutal reality of your own performance is extremely important for your growth and maturity as a professional.

*Flashback: Mr. Not Me, was asked to manage a technical group, even though he had no expertise with the particular products. He was told the team had enough expertise but that they lacked leadership that would enable them to make decisions and complete projects. Mr. Not Me took the job because he wanted to learn this new technology and help the company out.*

*After he took on the new job, projects continued to slip. Mr. Not Me employed all the tricks he knew to manage the projects and spent a lot of time talking to the team, but he was still unable to control the outcome. He was blaming everything and everyone else for the failure until one day, it hit him. He realized that it must be his own fault, because his team was full of intelligent people who apparently knew what they were doing.*

*The brutal reality was that the team resented the fact that he had not worked in that technology. Because of his lack of experience, they felt he was unqualified to lead the team. Obviously this was a painful reality for Mr. Not Me, but he had to face it in order to move on.*

One should always face the facts of a brutal reality with the faith that it can be fixed. It is meaningless to say that something is broken but have no desire or faith that it's fixable. So, Mr. Not Me had three choices: (1) don't change anything and probably fail; (2) leave the group/company; or (3) learn the technology of the group by asking its experts to tutor him, and by reading more. This last choice would have helped the manager establish credibility with the team and get the cooperation needed to complete the project—assuming he was given the time to train on the job.

The key point here is that one must face reality and pick a plan to move forward. Mr. Not Me chose option three, and although it took more than two years for the team to fully accept him as their leader, their overall performance finally improved. Leaders in technology companies must have both technical abilities and management abilities in order to succeed.

It is vitally important that leaders surface issues and launch a plan to solve them in a timely manner. Not facing reality is only postponing the inevitable, and resolving problems later on can be costly. Facing reality head-on—no matter how brutal—is always the smart choice. And in order to do that effectively, it's imperative that you know how to communicate.

# CHAPTER 3

# Communicate, Communicate, and Communicate Some More

Communication is one of the key issues in any organization. Management's job is to lay out a path to achieve the company's objectives and then clear that path of all obstacles. They must also create clear goals for each individual, because in order for people to succeed in the workplace, they need to have clear goals. The way managers lay out those goals is through active communication.

In my experience, organizations work more smoothly and productively when everyone knows what is going on. That means that everyone, from the top of the food chain to the bottom, should have full access to information. People work with more confidence and think with more clarity when they have information about their project, and they need to know more than the bare minimum. They have to have a complete idea not only of their goals but of the overall plan of attack. The clearer an individual's goal, the better chance he or she has of achieving it—as well as the larger objectives of the organization.

When project goals are not clear, people need to hear from management to achieve some degree of clarity. This is necessary because when people don't have information about the future, they experience discomfort and stress; it's human nature. In my experience, I have found that people always prefer hearing the reality regarding their projects—no matter how dire the situation,—over being kept in the dark.

At times, it's acceptable to communicate that even management does not know what the plan is, but that they are working on one. This simple communication removes a lot of anxiety and builds trust. And obviously, once the manager states that he doesn't know the plan, he needs to work quickly to determine one, even if it is only at a high level.

Often organizations fail to see the value of communication and don't train their managers to communicate effectively with their subordinates. This leads to severe inefficiencies and builds anxiety in the organization. Simple information, such as who is working on what task; which device or product will be available when; what the delivery dates are for key milestones; where documents can be found; where to find project status; where to find open issues; and the priorities of projects makes a huge difference in increasing efficiency by reducing confusion, questions, emails, etc.

It is inexcusable for managers not to encourage and enforce regular communication within the organization, especially with so much new technology at our disposal. With intranet technology, any organization can build their own portal (for example, an internal website for the company) and easily disseminate information about everything that is happening within a specific group or within the entire organization. I have seen very sophisticated portals with collaboration capabilities for organizations that share updated information in almost real time.

Once the portal has been built, organizations that embrace this type of strategy experience very efficient communication with only minimum pain required to update the content. These teams understand that the more people know, the more productive they will be. Using the portal as a gateway to information becomes a way of life.

A portal can also help ensure that duplication of effort is avoided. People use significant mental energy to solve problems, and it's a waste when there is duplication of effort by multiple teams to solve the same problem. In large organizations (50+ people), I've often seen individual contributors and managers start tasks without knowing that someone else had done the same task or was in the process of developing the same solution. Progress and solutions need to be clearly communicated.

In order to reduce duplication, management must clarify who is working on what and who the expert go-to people are for specific subject matters. I call these people "domain experts." In large organizations, it can be difficult to know who is an expert in what. This is especially true for newcomers. If the organization has grown slowly enough, old-timers may know who to go to in times of crisis. But if an organization grows fast, everyone will need to know who has what expertise and in which specific areas. One effective management action is to publish a "domain expertise list" to clarify who to go to with specific questions or issues.

I was in an organization where communication was so bad that people didn't know who to go for information related to their project. Even managers didn't know which way to point their subordinates. Because the managers didn't know who the domain experts were, they instructed the individual who asked the question to start learning the new domain and then solve the problem herself. This was good for the engineer and the manager—it meant they would eventually have their own expert in their group. But for the organization as a whole, this approach was inefficient; it discouraged sharing information for the greater good of the company and, in effect, duplicated effort needlessly.

This brings us to a parallel issue: management's responsibility to clarify the roles and responsibilities of individual team members. It is well established that most people don't like too many processes and rules to follow. However, roles, responsibilities, and process are all elements that fall under the greater umbrella of communication.

If people don't understand the role of all the relevant teams, management has failed to communicate those roles and is therefore creating ambiguity about who is doing what. Avoid assigning multiple names to be responsible for the same exact task. Similarly, in large or multi-project organizations, leaders need to communicate where each team's responsibility begins and ends to avoid overlap and unnecessary duplication.

Please note that I'm not advocating building excess bureaucracy—far from it. The point is that clear communication in all areas can only improve organizational efficiency. Be careful that you don't consume all of your team's time communicating at the expense of working on deliverables. A manager must always determine the appropriate balance of time between communicating tasks and individual work. If you have too many meetings or too many long meetings, for example, people will stop attending or fail to pay attention when they do.

There's a real need for managers to coach people on how to set up and chair meetings. Basic rules—such as having an agenda and sending meeting minutes (short, not a life story) consistently—are a minimum. I want to emphasize that a manager always needs to lead by example, and running meetings is one of the best places to exhibit exemplary leadership behavior. Unfortunately, most organizations are notoriously weak in communication, and the group's work efficiency suffers as a result.

*Flashback: One manager, Mr. Closed Mouth, didn't think communication was all that important. He would attend his supervisor's staff meetings and agree to pass information down to his own troops, but these turned out to be empty promises. Mr. Closed Mouth never held staff meetings with his own team because, in his opinion, meetings were a complete waste of the engineers' time.*

*As they say, nature abhors a vacuum. The engineers would hear things from different sources, try to put together what was happening, and usually end up getting it wrong. This was detrimental to the project because people had different assumptions about what was going on.*

In some cases, certain information may not be relevant to the engineers' work, but they're curious nonetheless. By communicating with them, a manager reduces anxiety, not to mention rumor and ambiguity. Managers must communicate as much as possible via many mediums regarding what is going on in the organization. I've found that managers who are poor communicators are oftentimes not effective because their team ends up inefficient and uncoordinated. Conversely, good communication *always* shows employees that a manager cares about them.

Part of the manager's job is to communicate priorities to the group. All teams, given their level of energy, intelligence, and related factors, have limits on their productivity. When too many projects stretch the capabilities of the team, the only choice is to prioritize and create new schedule estimates for the lower priority projects. This way, the organization makes sure that it addresses the highest priority projects with the necessary resources, and that it can with some certainty deliver these projects on time.

It is a leader's responsibility to let people know what not to do. The "not to do" list is as important as the "to do" list. There are always unreasonable folks who will tell you that all projects are equally high priority and must be completed on time. These people are often new to complex engineering projects, and will probably mature after they've lived through a few painful failures.

One of the most complex issues in management is estimating the effort required to complete projects, given the manpower available. This is a perennial issue for all managers who need to set reasonable deadlines while justifying dates to their superiors.

During the planning phase, good managers build credibility when they create schedule estimates. Healthy and mature organizations reach an understanding that everyone has done their best in pushing the organization to its entitlement limits. However, there are always more projects than available resources. Leaders must therefore understand the power of prioritization to keep all wheels turning at the right rate.

Prioritization helps people understand the sense of urgency on particular projects in order to maximize a specific business measurement-metric, such as profits or strategic positioning. Mature organizations understand that prioritization is inevitable, especially when working for an inexperienced leader and even when resources are not an issue at the time of prioritization. Unplanned events always occur; if priorities are not set, allocating the right people to the right projects becomes difficult. Regular, periodic communication is healthy and encourages a culture that respects priorities.

*Flashback: The engineering team at my company was overwhelmed with requests for too many projects. Marketing made everything high priority; every project was priority one. Worse, they claimed that failing to meet any of the projects would cause the company to collapse!*

*Marketing was frustrated with the engineering team for not being able to meet all the requests. The engineering team was frustrated with marketing's unreasonable demands and its inability to understand the limited number of people available to do all the work.*

*The issue here was on both sides. Marketing refused to understand the engineers' pain and resource limitations, and the engineering managers failed to justify their resource limitations with real data.*

*To solve the problem, the engineering managers collected all the data needed, such as the number of projects and who was working on what task. This was helpful in getting the marketing team to appreciate the workload. Eventually, marketing understood that if we stayed on the same path, some key projects would be impacted with severe repercussions. To avoid major slips in some of the "high revenue projects" they started prioritizing.*

*Moving step by step, we eventually established a clear prioritization of all projects and achieved far greater productivity as a result.*

Here's a tip from Management Psychology 101: managers must be careful when communicating priorities to their teams since no one likes to work on low-priority projects! There are several different approaches to this issue. Managers may keep the prioritization information to themselves but use it to make the right calls when faced with a resource conflict. Alternatively, they can share the information with the team and simply state that this is the reality of life. This method is most effective if the manager can simultaneously encourage the group and remind them that everyone will be rotated to higher-priority projects in the future.

Emails are another common source of communication failure. Some people don't write at all (one extreme), and others write more than they should (the other extreme). Some write extremely polite emails and others seem only to be able to say nasty things in theirs. As with everything else in life, one must seek a moderate position rather than default to extremes. I believe people can learn to revise their tendencies in just such a way.

I have successfully coached people with email problems by asking them to give themselves a fair evaluation. By changing their approach, how might they achieve improved results? I break things down by asking the manager to explain the goal of a particular email. Does it help anyone? Does it motivate people to work harder? Does it clarify the issue? If the answer is "no" to any of these questions, then the email is mostly likely doing the opposite—frustrating and demotivating people.

I highly recommend that managers at every level walk around and visit the troops as often as possible. This is an aspect of communication I call "physical presence." It's also referred to as "management by walking around." It is very important for the troops to see their leader and to talk with him or her.

In these interactions, everyone in the group should feel the freedom to talk about anything, even if it's not related to work, simply as a way to connect. However, a smart leader uses this time to reinforce key messages that everyone needs to hear. Another way leaders can accomplish this is by sending emails periodically to communicate the "state of the union" and to energize the organization as a whole. Also, regular "all hands" meetings are very effective and necessary in large organizations. The presenters in all hands meetings must ensure that people walk away *motivated* and informed with reality—or not have the meeting at all.

Communication becomes more difficult for organizations operating out of multiple sites; with physical distance, the flow of information is generally slower. It may also be difficult to get remote managers to comply with regular reporting deadlines.

Contrary to the intuition of most managers, the best way to deal with remote sites is to recognize up front that the number of metrics to be tracked and reported needs to be higher than those of a local site. This is because leaders cannot depend on visiting and talking to remotely located people as often. Remote sites often have a slightly different culture than the main corporate site, making it even harder to provide effective leadership.

This is why it is vital for managers operating at remote sites to be stronger, better trained, and more autonomous than their local (or "home") counterparts.

*Flashback: Mr. Long Distance Manager was asked to expand his US team to India. He decided to hire and manage the team directly from the US rather than hire a local manager. He went to India but refused to take advice from the local managers that already worked in the company, insisting that he wanted people to report directly to him.*

*Mr. Long Distance Manager did not understand the Indian culture and the process of hiring people in India. With the local HR's help he was able to hire ten people. Mr. Long Distance Manager was traveling to India every few months and was on the phone with them every day. After a year or so, four out of the 10 people he hired quit. Morale was low and productivity was low with this team.*

*Mr. Long Distance Manager learned the hard way that local managers are key in making remote sites successful. After spending lots of time interviewing and listening to the local managers, he finally hired a local manager. All communication issues and low productivity issues disappeared! The right local manager had worked with US teams and knew the local culture; therefore was able to lead the team with minimum supervision from Mr. Long Distance Manager.*

It is important to realize that managers have to be measured to a higher standard than individual contributors. If a manager is behaving to an extreme, others may follow his or her example. Before long, this behavior can easily spin out of control and become part of the company culture. For this reason, leaders must be extra careful with their behavior and not go to extremes in their positions.

*Flashback: Mr. Cause Pain was a director who caused pain to every department to complete his projects. His style was to embarrass people in public and bark loudly to make things happen. He was successful in completing projects on time and customers liked his products. Upper management liked him because he was successful in delivering results. As a matter of fact this director was promoted to a VP position in a short period of time. I was new to this company and still trying to figure out the culture and particularly Mr. Cause Pain. I learned quickly that his team was the major source of pain in my department. Mr. Cause Pain's direct reports were mimicking their boss's style thinking that behavior would help them get promotions. I later found out that Mr. Cause Pain's boss behaved similarly. This high tension culture did not last long since morale was getting lower and good people were leaving the company. Eventually, the VP left the company and productivity went up. As you can see, people learn from their leaders and good leaders know this.*

When there is a need to modify the behavior or culture of an organization, a leader should understand the doctrine of baby steps. Any behavior, whether it's of an individual or a group of people, is adopted gradually over a period of time; similarly, it takes a long time to alter it. Leaders must understand this and not expect change to come overnight.

To modify a culture or behavior, build a long-term plan. For example, you might decide to develop a four-year measurable roadmap of quarterly baby steps. It is extremely important that the entire management team and all the individual contributors buy into the "baby steps roadmap." In my experience, people are more receptive to change presented in this manner than any other management technique targeting change.

People are okay with change if they know it is not going to happen overnight—as long as the plan is clearly defined and agreed upon by all people prior to implementation. Most important, the team knows not to go on to the next baby step unless (and until) the previous baby steps have been completed and internalized. I have used this methodology in two different companies with excellent results.

Leaders cannot point their fingers in one direction and expect the company and the team to blindly march that way. They must outline baby steps and hold the group's hand along the way. Also, leaders cannot write one huge document stating what needs to be done (e.g., a new process) and expect the team to follow it immediately. These tactics fail miserably. Instead, leaders must understand the doctrine of baby steps as the most effective way to modify deeply ingrained behaviors.

People accept small changes but have a harder time with big ones. Over time, the accumulation of small changes makes people feel like they are part of the transformation, which results in the big change that was the original goal.

A leader's communication skill is paramount for his or her success. This is especially important in technology companies because everything moves so much faster than in other types of businesses. Managers who are poor communicators plateau quickly. As a good leader, you must communicate well not only with your subordinates but with your peers, your superior and upper management, and must contribute to what we'll discuss in the next chapter: the greater good.

CHAPTER 4

# Look for the Greater Good

In my younger days, I was naive enough to think that all you needed for a successful startup company was for great engineers to develop a great product; the rest of the organization was irrelevant. How wrong I was! True leaders go beyond the call of duty in their commitment to passionately pursue the greater good of the company. That means that their focus goes beyond their individual group or department to encompass the organization as a whole.

In order for a company to succeed, every department must do extremely well, especially when the company (or new product) is in its infancy phase. An organization succeeds when all departments achieve their goals, not just when one or two departments are successful. A perfect example of this occurred in the 1970s when video tape recorders were introduced. The Beta tape player had a much better technical performance than the VHS system, but it didn't become a standard because of a failure in marketing. If marketing and engineering had worked together, they could have changed the path of at-home entertainment as we know it.

*Flashback: I once worked at a startup company where the engineers thought that if the product was engineered well and they understood the customers' needs, then the product would sell itself without the help of the marketing department.*

*At the end of the program, we had a well-engineered product, but the company still failed, for two reasons: (1) the product was missing several features that were critical to customer acceptance (due to a marketing disconnect); and (2) even though some customers were happy with the feature set, we couldn't produce the product because the procurement department hadn't ordered the right parts on time.*

*By the time we were able to ship the product, it was too late; we were beaten out by a competitor and missed the market window.*

*Here's the moral of the story: ALL departments must be running at full speed to make a company successful, especially in startup situations. Even in the best of situations, it's all too easy for companies to fail due to market conditions, customer image, or just plain bad luck.*

It is sad but true that many managers and senior individual contributors don't understand the value of doing the right thing for the greater good. In my experience, a large percentage of people never fully grasp this concept. They don't care what happens to other departments in the organization, as long as their own group looks good.

*Flashback: One newly appointed marketing manager in a start up company, Mr. Bad Mouth, had a habit of bad-mouthing everyone but himself. He blamed every mistake or delay in the schedule on engineering management. Meanwhile, he ignored the fact that he himself kept changing the requirements of the products every week and insisting that they would be worthless unless the new features were added.*

*In addition to his lack of maturity, Mr. Bad Mouth had a dominating personality and often threw tantrums when he didn't get his way or when he was blamed for making the product late. The worst kind of manager, he was a constant source of demoralization for the team, and he failed to understand that he needed to work with other departments to help them succeed. Mr. Bad Mouth blamed the engineers for every mistake instead of working cooperatively toward achieving the company's goals.*

*One way to view this scenario is as a failure of senior management for not recognizing the issue; they could have and perhaps should have intervened by attempting to develop the maturity of the marketing manager. The next level of management needed to explain to him that he was causing great harm by failing to focus on the greater good.*

*Unfortunately, that didn't happen. Upper management saw this manager as forceful and knowledgeable, and they couldn't see what he was doing to the morale of the entire organization until it was too late.*

The greater good applies to all levels of the organization: individual contributors, managers, directors, VPs, teams, departments, business units, and companies. All members of a team or organization should help others in times of need so that the entire team will succeed. Having one part done perfectly while the rest of the project lags behind is counterproductive.

Leaders must encourage an environment where people can shine *while also* encouraging them to help others. Leaders need to let their subordinates know that they will be measured on two elements: personal performance and contributions to the greater good. Work is like a basketball game—one player may be fantastic, but if he is selfish, the team may still lose.

*Flashback: I had two managers who were both type-A personalities and very ambitious to move up the ladder. They had different roles and responsibilities, but they needed each other to complete their projects. One manager's job was to deliver the hardware, and the other's job was to deliver the software for the project.*

*The issue was that they were always competing with one another at the expense of the project. Both constructed their designs and did their work separately, as if they were on different islands. Because each one assumed that he knew everything that needed to be done, the hardware manager delivered his magnificent hardware, thinking it was perfect, and the software manager delivered her flawless software, thinking it was the greatest thing since sliced bread. But once we put them together, it was a total disaster!*

*Thanks to their personalities and oversized egos, the project suffered. They wasted countless hours on the blame game. Obviously, no one was winning in this situation.*

*I spent a significant amount of time with each of them; then worked with them together, and I still could not succeed in solving the issue. Finally, I was able to get them to work together as a team by telling them that they would both be measured on the total project, regardless of their individual deliveries. In other words, both would be rewarded only if the total project was successful. That meant that if one of them failed, they both failed.*

*At first they objected to the concept, arguing that an individual can only control his or her own group. But after some back and forth, during which time I held firm to my position on how they were going to be measured, they completely changed their attitude toward each other.*

*The subsequent projects were an order of magnitude more successful than the previous ones. While the two managers continued to compete with one another, they were now competing on who helped the other team more—a competition I encourage and reward.*

Often the best way to have leaders focus on the greater good is to tie their compensation to the success of the entire company, not just their own group. Stock options accomplish this by making people stakeholders in the company. Short-term individual goals can be tied to a specific incentive, but larger incentives should always be driven by the overall success of the company. Creating these kinds of incentives as a part of your business process will take some time. But the more you do it, the better at it you'll get.

I believe that leaders must become selfless. Some would argue that most managers in high positions got there because they have big egos. This may be true, but I contend that many of these managers won't be able to sustain their success or their company's success for long without embracing the greater good principle.

So, regardless of how you got to your position, make a habit of improving yourself, your team, and helping the people around you. Which leads us directly to the next principle of effective leadership: always improve on what you've got.

C H A P T E R   5

# Promote Improvements Relentlessly

You've probably heard the saying, "If it ain't broke, don't fix it." This axiom couldn't be more flawed! Leaders must find a way to constantly improve everything the organization is doing. If you wait until something is broken to make improvements, it's often too late to fix it—and it is always more costly.

*Flashback: Our Company had good products that were very competitive, and life was good. But one day we heard that the competition's product was performing 20 percent better than ours. We immediately bought a sample and tested it to see what they were doing. To our surprise, we discovered that they weren't using components that were any more expensive than ours. Rather, this competitor had found a way to improve their product performance by using better algorithms (software) in their products, without adding any cost.*

*This was a huge disruption to our sales and marketing team, and the entire company was affected. It was the wakeup call our company leaders needed to change the way we operated. Up to that point, their motto had always been: "Let's not invest dollars; business is just fine, and we want to control cost." Essentially, the notion that if it wasn't broken it didn't need to be fixed had long formed the backbone of the company philosophy.*

*There's an old joke that goes like this: a person was falling from the Empire State Building. Every time he passed by a floor, he would say "So far, so good." But suddenly—splat! The floors bottomed out onto nothing but concrete. The moral of the story is: just because you haven't hit the ground yet doesn't mean you're safe!*

*Fortunately for our company, we avoided a similar fate. We were able to gather the best brains of the company together and improve our performance. The recovery took nine months, which was costly, but finally we were able to compete in the marketplace again.*

Leaders must constantly push the organization to improve. This is especially true in hi-tech companies where the axiom usually is, "If you are not moving forward, you are falling behind." Of course, anyone who has ever worked in a hi-tech company knows this is more easily said than done. In order to succeed, every manager in the company must understand this concept and actually put the policy into practice.

One way of ensuring this dynamic is to develop a process that creates periodic discomfort. This discomfort is designed to drive constant improvements in the basic way the company conducts its business. For example, establishing periodic roadmap reviews for every important aspect of the business is one way to institutionalize constant improvement. Another solution is to make sure that there are quantitative measurements in place for each element. With measurements in place, you can plan and track your progress over time.

Each manager needs to identify these key elements: cost, cycle time, quality, technology, performance, size, market share, and response time. Then he or she must establish quantitative measurements for each of these elements. The leaders in the organization should be able to navigate their improvement programs by just looking at a dashboard of these parameters and continuously improve the metric, refine the accuracy of the measurement, or add new measurements that better reflect the key needs of the business.

It is essential that every manager in the organization feels the responsibility to constantly improve on the processes he or she is overseeing, keeping in mind the competitive advantage of the company's key product offerings. Constantly improving the product or the company's processes cannot be delegated to just one person. For example, although product definition is usually the primary responsibility of marketing, the engineering staff must understand the details of competitors' products as well, and be encouraged to share their knowledge.

Engineers can work in the background, creating new ideas that will ensure the company's competitive edge. One very effective approach is to assign the engineering team the responsibility of reverse engineering competitors' products. The team may then create cost estimates of these products and forecast each competitor's likely follow-up products or improvements.

Instead of succumbing to the urge to focus on daily fire-fighting, leaders should concentrate their energies on building their dashboards and training the management team to use them. More often than not, I see leaders filling their time with activities that I'm sure they believe are urgent; meanwhile, they never find the time to build the dashboards that drive improvement. Does this require more effort and time to do? Yes. But establishing key metrics and creating a culture of constant improvement should be a top priority.

Managers need to focus on tactical day-to-day tasks while also focusing on long-term strategic improvements and competitiveness. This includes the competitiveness of their own products, as well as the process by which their company develops, manufactures, and markets these products. Improvements in these areas have vast potential. For example, what would happen if one of the competitors used a new tool that cut two months off the development schedule for every future product? You can imagine how adding this improvement to your own business would affect the company's bottom line!

Some people like to do things because they have a gut feeling based on their experience. However, following a gut feeling can end up being a waste of time, or even an all-out disaster if the feeling turns out to be wrong. Furthermore, people resent following a plan without understanding the logic behind the decision (gut feelings are hard to explain logically).

While a leader's gut feeling can be important, even valuable, it needs to be backed up with a reasonable percentage of real data. This is why leaders must create a data-driven culture. It is important to educate team members in the meaning and expectations of a data-driven work environment. This doesn't mean that you must operate with 100 percent data, 100 percent of the time. Good leaders know when to act with partial data—say, when they have 60 percent of the information needed to make a particular decision. Waiting for 100 percent of the data can sometimes do more damage than good and can make an organization slower than its competitors or make an organization miss a key market opportunity.

Solid data is generally more important for making strategic decisions than tactical ones. Tactical decisions are short-term and can often be made based on a gut feeling, though they still need to be backed up with enough information to help sell the decision to the internal team. Strategic decisions, on the other hand, require more hard data, because you must have a thorough understanding of the competition and the long-term trends of your industry before launching your plan of attack.

43

When it comes to improving or establishing new processes, do the minimum. Keep it simple and your plan might actually get used. Unfortunately, some managers use Microsoft Project to run everything; they build very detailed plans that only they can understand. After a few weeks, these plans diverge from reality and the manager spends all his or her time keeping the plans up-to-date. If the plans are updated too often, people stop believing in them.

Keep your plans simple; otherwise they become obsolete. Make sure everyone can comprehend them, and that your team has the desire to contribute. Keep your objectives maintainable so that everyone can happily engage to keep the work current and meaningful. People have to perceive your process improvements and measurements as a tool that will actually save them time versus a chore that will only mean additional work.

Technology leaders create *disciplined engineering cultures*. A disciplined culture is when people stop for a red traffic light even when they don't see any police cars. Most engineers know the correct process to do things beyond just technical capabilities. Examples: They know that a design is not complete without proper documentation. They know that one must write design specifications before jumping into implementation. They also know that every development must be tested before declaring that it is complete. Sometimes this common sense disappears under time pressure. Leaders must create and encourage an environment where engineers are naturally disciplined to do the right things without the need for lengthy procedural policies. This can only be accomplished when the leader accepts the fact that sometimes the right thing to do may cost more in dollars or time. From my experience, disciplined organizations that focue on the correct process are more efficient and more productive than the undisciplined ones that often rely on heroics and fire-fighting. Therefore, it should never cost more to do the right things when you are in a disciplined environment.

Leaders must constantly look for improvements in all areas of their domain and beyond their domain. As a leader you must relentlessly identify areas that need improvement and create simple plans to address them. Then, as we'll discuss in the next chapter, you must follow through and execute your plans to completion.

CHAPTER 6

# Follow Through on Everything

Every manager's goal is to successfully execute his or her plan. Of course, as we all know, the devil is in the details!

Leaders are responsible for ensuring that all departments are executing as planned and that surprises are minimized. A leader must follow through on all objectives he or she takes on while staying close enough to the project details to make sure that everyone else is following through on their commitments. I'm not suggesting that leaders should micro-manage their people. Rather, leaders need to have mechanisms in place to ensure that the key plans and strategies are actually getting executed.

Some leaders are naturally detail-oriented and others are not. It is critical that you know your own strengths and weaknesses. There's nothing new here—to thine own self be true—you need to be honest and identify your own shortcomings. If you are not into the low-level details, then make sure your generals are sufficiently detail-oriented as a way to compensate. Great leaders will identify their personal weak points and surround themselves with subordinates who can make the overall endeavor a success.

In control systems theory, you must be able to measure the thing that you are trying to control. The same theory is applicable to leading a business or a project or a team. To ensure that plans are being executed, *define* their key elements and establish periodic check points or milestones. Clearly identify for the team what progress looks like to you. Then establish progress reports—paper or electronic, and, wherever possible, in person—and explain that everyone is required to participate.

It is very effective to have each participant regularly share a report with the rest of the senior team. For example, perhaps each senior manager issues an email progress report every Friday night. This helps establish, through example, the usefulness of formal reporting. Also, peer pressure will encourage everyone to continue to keep the communication flowing. Nobody wants to be the one person who didn't get their progress report in—the weakest link of the chain. This helps reinforce the notion that every senior team member is responsible to share progress with every other senior team member, not just to the boss.

It is also important to *act* on the information provided. If the manager's reaction is too slow or is incorrect, the plan may spin out of control and the project could fail. I've seen many managers make the mistake of failing to identify the elements that need to be measured. Erecting standards of measurement can be time-consuming, and many managers justify their negligence by saying, "There just isn't time." At the other end of the spectrum, I've seen managers take the time to identify the correct items to be tracked—but then forget to regularly track their progress!

Please note that the standards of measurement I am referring to are not Microsoft Project "tasks." The items you need to track are a higher level; these are often items you have measured on previous projects. You may even have historical data to draw upon that can help with your planning estimates. Use this previous data wherever possible.

*Flashback: Presenting Mr. Not FollowUp, a VP of a large engineering organization who talked more than he listened. He gave orders in meetings and in emails to all his direct reports. Mr. Not FollowUp was a brilliant technologist who came up the ranks on the strength of his technical knowledge. He would give plenty of instructions to his team on what to do and how things should be done, was very thorough in his plans, and expected people just to implement what he asked for.*

*One morning Mr. Not FollowUp called an emergency meeting and invited all his direct reports. He told them that a key customer had dropped them as a vendor because of the failings of his direct reports.*

*The bottom line was that the product had multiple fatal bugs that would require six months to fix. These fatal bugs could have been avoided if the team had done some of the things Mr. Not FollowUp had demanded months earlier. Mr. Not FollowUp was surprised that his team had not followed through. On one hand, his inexperienced direct reports should have followed their boss's instructions but on the other hand, the buck stops at the big boss. Mr. Not FollowUp should have set up a mechanism to make sure his instructions were followed through. A simple tracking system and periodic reviews would have made this disaster avoidable. This was a hard lesson for Mr. Not FollowUp.*

Sometimes knowing what to measure is a matter of experience. For instance, prior to the release of a product, a leader may decide to measure the frequency with which design changes are being submitted by the engineering team. Here, a product can be anything that has a clearly defined output, such as building a device or releasing a software package. If the number of changes is higher than the historical data, it means the risk is higher for discovering additional problems in the product. The best course of action may be to not release the product until the frequency of changes is reasonably small. Another way to minimize risk is to reduce the number of features that the product will support at its initial release.

Reacting to project issues in a timely fashion is vitally important. It is the leader's job to anticipate that bad things happen all the time, and then to avoid or miti-gate them in a timely manner. You cannot afford to wait until the train hits the wall to start applying corrective action. The leader must change direction if necessary by anticipating where the train will go if nothing is done to stop it.

Some managers react to schedule problems by sim-ply working harder and demanding longer hours, hop-ing to avoid the train wreck. Although it is true that working hard may have an impact on the final outcome, making minor course corrections early on in the project can often save the train from crashing in the first place. It is the leader's job to see disaster coming before any-one else and to take preventive action early enough to ensure that the project avoids it on its path to success.

Even if leaders cannot measure every metric at every second, they must have access to sufficient progress feedback at all times. They must also possess the good judgment to know when to intervene. Depending on the situation, you may need to increase or decrease the frequency of measurement reporting. Looking at the dashboard once a month may be sufficient, but it may be necessary to check it every hour when crisis strikes. Obviously, if the frequency needs to be high all the time, this is an indication that something is wrong and that perhaps the leaders below you are not well-trained. In this situation, you must decide whether to continue coaching those below you or to find individuals who are more capable.

Leaders who don't follow through get a lot of surprises. Some managers get upset at the team's performance instead of owning up to their own failures to plan, measure, and correct problems. To paraphrase P.T. Barnum, "You can track some of the metrics for project success all of the time and you can track all of the metrics for project success some of the time, but you cannot measure all the metrics for project success all of the time."

Leaders follow through on their plans and encourage their direct reports to follow through on their commitments by establishing a fair rewarding system, which we'll discuss in the next chapter as another key element of leadership.

# CHAPTER 7

# Reward People Fairly and Consistently

Everyone likes to be rewarded. When the first Stone Age hunter brought the spoils of his hunt to the village, I'm sure the happy locals rewarded him by letting him take the first cut while dancing in his honor and putting a feather or two in his hair. As that same hunter brought more meat to the village, he no doubt received additional recognition—perhaps a more colorful feather or a new cave with a view.

But perhaps at some point the hunter felt that he had paid his dues and no longer needed to hunt. After a long time of not bringing home the bacon (quite literally), the decorated hunter probably no longer enjoyed the recognition and the respect he had once received. Those rewards hadn't just made the hunter feel good; they encouraged him to go out and hunt some more.

That Stone Age village was sending a message to all the individuals in the tribe: we reward hunters who deliver. The tribe most likely repeated this recognition as new hunters brought home their kill. The mechanisms for identifying and rewarding became a tradition. In today's workplace, we call this the "compensation focal process."

Back in the Stone Age, individuals who didn't bring anything to the table were most likely the freeloaders who got only the scraps after everyone else was done eating.

The world has not changed much after 65,000 years of evolution. People today expect to be rewarded both for their individual contributions and their team's successes. They expect similar promotions, merit increases, and bonuses for the same scope of accomplishments. People also want rewards to be consistent across the organization and expect that all individuals who accomplish similar tasks will be similarly rewarded.

Furthermore, people expect rewards to be fair. Rewards should be given without prejudice or favoritism based on personal relationships or other factors, such as belonging to the same club, sharing an education level, or for reasons of sex, race, country of origin, or religion. In other words, the reward must depend only on the accomplishment of the individual, not on who the individual is or what the overall team may have accomplished in the past.

In the title of this chapter—"Reward people fairly and consistently"—the word "fairly" turns out to be the most difficult one to follow. This is because leaders are human and emotions can cloud their judgment. Even if things are in fact "fair," it is easy to leave the impression that favoritism played a role in a reward situation if the

manager is not careful to cultivate an appropriate reputation for fairness.

Perhaps you're thinking: Aren't businesses more
profitable if they don't have to worry about rewarding
people? Fewer rewards mean more money for the company to keep, right? This thinking may be correct in the
short term, but its dead wrong in the long term. Businesses use rewards to energize the organization and to
send a message to all employees that the results from
smart, hardworking people will be rewarded consistently and fairly. This is the universal way of doing business,
and it's beautiful.

Leaders must use this tool wisely. Without it, employees can easily become demotivated, which can kill key
projects. Over time, inconsistency in recognition and
rewards will contaminate the organization. Once the
members of an organization know that, for whatever
reason, there are inconsistencies in recognition, the
integrity of the leader will be tarnished. That loss of
reputation is very hard to repair.

Let's talk about the "old boys' club" mentality. I've
seen this in almost every company I've worked for. Often
these individuals share a common denominator—they
may be among the first fifty people in a startup company, a group of founders, or the team that built the
company's first product. They could also be the team
in a department that stuck together through bad financial times, or the team that helped build a new remote
site from scratch or won a big account. Naturally, these
people were extremely important at the time when the
company needed them.

However, leaders must understand that, in order for long-term growth to happen, companies must evolve and the business must grow. That means that new people will be added. The leaders have to keep fueling the entrepreneurial spirit while at the same time integrating and energizing the *entire* organization.

I've heard founding employees complain that without them, there would be no company, and they ought to be given special treatment forever. This management problem must be addressed by leaders who recognize its invisible but insidious effect on the new members of the team. But you don't want to isolate your old members, either; you may very well want to keep as many of the original contributors as possible, especially since they have the "genetic information" about what has worked in the past.

And yet, the last thing a leader wants to do is to allow disengaged employees to poison overall morale with stories of how things were better in the "good old days." Sometimes original team members have been superb contributors and have given a lot to the company. But all their wisdom and knowledge is useless if it can't be harvested productively in the present.

I've seen many early contributors grow with the company. I've also known individuals who have failed to mature personally while everyone else—and the company—moved ahead. It is highly disruptive to the organization when management is afraid to disturb the old boys' club and fails to initiate corrective action with these individuals. It takes true leaders to manage this type of situation. First, recognize the individuals who understand that companies can't have two classes and want to transition the company to a more mature organization. Second, energize these individuals to infect the old boys' club with a passion to mature. Third, monitor progress, just as you would in any important project. And fourth, send home the individuals who refuse to understand the big picture—regardless of their position.

Good leaders promote the deserving people when they are ready and when there is a need in the company. They don't wait for the employee to ask for it. Too often, people have to complain to their manager before getting a promotion. It is far better if the promotion comes without being solicited, but this can only happen when leaders value their subordinates and give the promotion at the right time. Unfortunately, very few leaders do this.

Leaders need to set goals that contain unambiguous expectations. Expectations and subsequent promotions for each level in the organization must be consistently defined to ensure clarity and understanding among managers. Some managers use subjective qualifications, and their personal relationships with their subordinates may cloud their judgment when it comes to promotions. One antidote to this is for the leader to review all promotions in the presence of all peer managers. I recommend garnering acceptance and buy-in from key managers before announcing any promotion.

A leader's key job is to energize his or her organization. Rewarding fairly and consistently is definitely a strong energizer, whereas failing to do so is a strong demotivator. By treating your people fairly and rewarding them for a job well done, you'll build a team that is eager to do their best work at all times.

> *Flashback: Mr. Equal Raises, a director at a high-pressure engineering company, gives equal raises to all his direct reports. Mr Big boss gave full discretion to all his direct reports to distribute our annual focal for our teams as long as we stayed within our budgets. Mr. Equal Raises, announced that he was planning to give equal raises to all of his direct reports, as he has done before. I asked him, why all the same? His answer was very disappointing! He said "It's easy and everyone gets something!" Then he added that "everyone is working equally hard anyway"! This type of rewarding system demotivates the top performers and does not encourage the low performers to do better. In fact, his team was a lower-performing team compared to the rest of the organization. It is important to reward top performers in proportion to their contributions and to not reward the low performers.*

Leaders must treat their team members fairly and consistently. Taking care of your team is your number one job as a leader. Caring for and maturing your team—the single most important ingredient in your success—is very important, as we'll discuss in the next chapter.

# CHAPTER 8

# Understand That the Right People Are Your Best Assets

Leaders should primarily focus on leading people, which includes hiring the right people for the roles that takes maximum advantage of their skills, ambitions, and desires. Hiring the right people comes first. Products and factories come second.

Strong organizations are made up of people who can climb the highest mountain. Weak organizations, on the other hand, are full of people who can accidentally burn the barn down. Without great people, every company will eventually fail, no matter how great the plan or how much money is available.

The output of any organization is only as good as the people in it. This may seem obvious, but not all leaders make hiring quality people a top priority. Managers often hire warm bodies under pressure and feel a sense of accomplishment when they meet their hiring plan—without serious regard to the quality of the people they've brought on board. I've even met managers who, as a practice, won't hire people who are smarter than they are!

There are myriad ways in which managers rationalize their inadequate hiring procedures. Perhaps they want to ensure that they will always be the top dog in the kennel and that no one will be able to replace them. Maybe the decision is based purely on ego, or on the desire to mentor somebody younger and less experienced. I once had a manager tell me that he wouldn't hire someone who said in the initial interview that he would want to change some things if he got the job. The hiring manager was afraid that this new hire would cause trouble by demanding changes!

Good hiring managers, however, should welcome positive change and not just hire "yes men."

Successful leaders always try to find the best possible people, preferably those with experiences that can help the organization improve. Good leaders *look* for people who are smarter than they are. They look for people who can challenge their own ways, seeking out people who are not afraid of change or who initiate change.

Good managers also know how to place the right people in the right positions. Having a very technical person with poor management skills in a managerial position is a huge disservice to the individual, his or her subordinates, and the company as a whole. The same is true when you have a non-technical person performing highly technical management.

*Flashback: Ms. Wrong Seat, a manager with good technical experience, was having some trouble running a very complex technical product development team in our company. So I offered her the opportunity to switch jobs and take another function in the organization managing modeling and simulations.*

*After some hesitation, she accepted the new position and did extremely well in the new role, delivering far beyond my (and her own) expectations. This manager was a high-caliber individual who belonged in the company but was just in the wrong position.*

*In the end, Ms. Wrong Seat was happier, her previous group was relieved, her new group was thrilled, and the organization overall was far more productive as a result.*

Strong leaders know that having the right people in the right seats is a large part of their job. They also know that great people tremendously improve the chances of success, even when the company decides to go in an entirely different direction.

*Flashback: I once joined a company where a product was being developed for a new market. I was a very young manager, eager to take on the world. On my first day, I met my new team of six engineers and discovered that none of them had done this type of engineering work before!*

*I was shocked. Surely there had been some kind of mistake—or at the very least a misunderstanding.*

*I made an appointment with the VP of engineering and explained to him the team's lack of experience. To my surprise, he said, "There is no mistake! We hired you because you are an expert in this technology and I know you can train our engineers in this new field."*

*I pointed out that it would be faster if we just hired people who had the necessary experience. He surprised me again by explaining that we couldn't let good people go just because of a change in product or market. He readily explained that these guys were very accomplished engineers who were loyal to the company and could be trained.*

*I hadn't considered this perspective, but took the challenge head on. I started training the engineers and managing the project to the best of my ability. The VP was absolutely right; the team was very bright and eager to learn new things. After training the team in the new technology, we not only delivered the product on time, but some of the team members became experts and went on to accomplish cutting-edge innovations in the field!*

Another point worth mentioning is that organizations should allow, enable, and encourage people to rotate positions within the company. This will keep morale up and help individuals to eventually find the place where they can contribute the most to the company's overall success.

Team members want to be acknowledged and treated as professionals. They want their team as a whole to be recognized as a professional contributor to the organization. In order to make that happen, leaders must create a culture where professionalism is expected, rewarded, and allowed to flourish. This means people must treat each other with respect and only bring up differences in a constructive and professional manner.

There are certain behaviors in a company's culture that are not appropriate. Name-calling, mudslinging, misrepresentation of facts, backstabbing, mutiny, and blackmailing should never be allowed; these behaviors must be dealt with immediately and severely. These are very real issues that occur in corporate America every day, even from highly educated people.

Part of maintaining the best people for your organization means weeding out those who do not conduct themselves with respect and integrity. If there are people on your team who cannot behave ethically, ask them to fix their behavior. If nothing changes, they must be asked to leave. People will test the boundaries of acceptable behavior—it's human nature. For this reason, it's crucial that managers create an atmosphere of professionalism and that they hold individuals accountable for their actions.

No one should be allowed to create chaos or destroy morale in any organization. It is unacceptable to allow anyone to misrepresent facts or purposely alienate other workers. People who insist on lowering the expected standards of professional behavior do not belong on the team; they will eventually undermine its productivity and overall success. It is the manager's responsibility to remove these people from the organization.

There is no substitute for intelligence and good attitude. Good employees are people who excel in their area of expertise and work hard to make things happen in the short term. And to make meaningful contributions in the long run, people need to be good human beings who want to make the world a better place.

Whenever you can, hire top talent who fit your company's core values; find them the right positions (seats) in the organization; nurture and help them mature; then get out of their way and let them excel.

In the next chapter, we're going to talk about how to continually encourage your team to achieve greater results by stretching themselves beyond what they thought they were capable of—and into a whole new realm of results.

# CHAPTER 9

# Stretch Goals

Leaders challenge their organization when they commit themselves and their teams to stretching goals. These goals may make your stomach churn at first, but with some good planning, paired with creative problem-solving tactics, they're feasible in the long run. Just remember, your competition is not standing idle, waiting for you to pass them.

Challenging an organization in this way imparts high energy to its members and brings about new and improved ways of doing things. If, for example, a development process historically took eight weeks to complete, a leader may ask to push the target closer to six weeks as a stretch goal. Although initially people may complain, when motivated and pushed, they often figure out amazing new ways to achieve things that seemed impossible before. I've seen this happen over and over again.

A side note here: I'm not advocating that you set impossible goals that defy physics. If an airport is 60 miles away, for example, and it takes an hour to get there without traffic, it is unrealistic and dangerous to stretch the goal and ask a taxi driver to get you there in ten minutes.

There are many ways to build schedules to meet goals. One method is to use historical data and prior experience to factor in complexity, staffing, and the quality requirements of the project deliverables. Even the most experienced managers can only state the best-case scenario, nominal scenario, and worst-case scenario for any given project. If you present many scenarios for a project, more often than not management will pick the best-case scenario with the shortest time.

Leaders pick goals that challenge every team member and then stretch these goals to a point that may make people uneasy. That's okay—a little bit of discomfort is a good thing. What's important is to strike a balance. Leaders understand not to pick unreasonable goals that stretch expectations too far. In other words, it's good to say, "Let's strive for the impossible, but let's not ask for the ridiculous!"

In 1962, President John F. Kennedy said, "We choose to go to the moon in this decade." Most people at the time thought it was impossible, but America achieved that goal with great difficulty and hard work. The point is: leaders must always push the envelope and challenge their teams. Otherwise, the competition will pass them.

*Flashback: I remember a large engineering review meeting in which the entire team was discussing how to improve a product performance by 10 percent.*

*The team was struggling, and after hours of different proposals and discussions, the VP said "I've changed my mind. I want you to find a way to improve performance by 10 X!"*

*The team did not know if the VP was trying to be funny or had simply lost his mind. However, it soon became very clear that he was serious. Just to make sure we were all on the same page, he said, "This is a long-term goal and I want you to go out and come back with a proposal to improve the performance by 10X."*

*Given the proper time frame, the team took the request seriously. After eight weeks of brainstorming, we came back with many proposals for different levels of performance improvements. As a matter of fact, the 10 percent improvement option was now a trivial matter! The 10X proposal required more investment up front but would achieve the goal and cost targets in the long run.*

*Strategically, the VP decided to move forward with the 10X proposal as an advanced development project. Tactically, we picked the option that met the marketing goals for that year.*

*The 10X project was launched three years after the original discussion and indeed changed the way the products were built in the industry. The point here is that stretch goals push the human mind to achieve things that seemed impossible at first, and an organization can't help but benefit as a result.*

Effective scheduling is fundamental to creating and achieving stretch goals. One of the most difficult questions in management is how to predict schedules, especially when they involve a large number of people and new (or evolving) technologies.

*Flashback: My managers once told me that they couldn't show me a schedule because they were counting on a few miracles to happen to complete the project. My response was: "Please show me your plan and indicate when the miracles must happen in order to meet the schedule!"*

*After some struggle, the managers were able to come up with the plan. We were able to assign each "miracle" to a team leader who would in turn drive a group of individuals to accomplish the task. This mitigated the complexity of the operation and eliminated the need for desperate prayer. The crux of the matter was really just a matter of finding the right resources to attack the problems.*

*The schedule was eventually modified to accommodate the complexity of the tasks while retaining the stretch goals and challenging everyone to perform to the best of their ability. Although the project was completed three months late, the result was an audacious and groundbreaking product that left the competition in the dust for years.*

Leaders use the "AND" function instead of the "OR" function when it comes to stretching goals. Here is a simple example: a manager asks an engineer to complete a task by a certain date and the engineer responds by saying I can only do the design OR the documentation by that date. Which one would you like me to do, the design OR the document? Manager's proper response is this: a disciplined engineer should design AND complete documentation before declaring a task is done. Please come up with a date to provide the design AND the document. From my experience, in some cases this AND function required more time to complete but in many cases it did not.

Obviously, you don't want to run your organization on extreme stretch goals all the time. Choose your battles wisely. You must pick the most important projects—the "biggest bang for the buck" projects—and stretch those goals. When you've met your goals, reward your team fairly and consistently.

If the goal is not fully met, reward your team to some extent, but not as much as if they had achieved the goal. In this way, you are acknowledging all their hard work and saying it is acceptable to sometimes miss stretch goals—as long as everyone gave it their all. This will create a culture that expects and even looks forward to stretch goals.

Success in this area can only be achieved when everyone in the organization understands that the project has stretch goals *and* will do whatever it takes to make them happen. A key point to keep in mind is that if you are meeting all of your schedules on time, you are probably not pushing hard enough to differentiate yourself from the competition. If you stretch your goals, you'll watch your productivity improve exponentially.

Once you've outlined your stretch goals, all that remains is for you to commit to them. This brings us to our tenth and final leadership principle: commitment.

# CHAPTER 10

# Value Commitment

Most people get nervous when committing to something that involves the unknown. It's human nature to feel discomfort when faced with something new. Commitment means making an agreement with one's self or among two or more people to face that fear and actually *do* something. When a person commits to a goal or project, his or her integrity is on the line.

A person can commit to himself to going to the gym every day. A person can make a commitment to stop smoking. A person can make a commitment to completing his project on time and say that people can count on it. All of these things are worthy commitments. Committing is almost like creating a contract: "I shall do this by this date." Any person with high integrity—a value all leaders should have—who fails to meet a commitment will feel a sense of loss and will understand that he or she has lost respect in the eyes of others. And if a person fails to meet commitments several times, then the person's words are simply no longer as meaningful.

In business, as in life, committing and delivering to your coworkers, subordinates, superiors, vendors, and customers is absolutely crucial. You must choose your words carefully, say what you intend to do, and do what you say. You've got to be ready to walk the talk. Leaders who realize the importance of commitment will expect their subordinates to respect their own commitments in return. If everyone in an organization respects commitment, the organization will be self-propelled, becoming a highly motivated work environment.

You don't have to use the word "commit" to enable this culture. All it requires is putting more emphasis on rewarding people who do whatever it takes to meet goals and deliver. In the case of low-performing individuals, a commitment culture will expose and expunge them naturally. Delivering on your commitments applies to both the big things (delivering a product on time) and the little things ("I'll email that report to you as soon as I get back to my desk"). This is how reputation and trust are built in all types of relationships.

I mentioned that a culture that values commitment is self-propelled. Once the leader commits to certain objectives, the subordinates are propelled to sign up to ensure that their leader can achieve them. Just remember to keep in mind that you should never take things to an extreme. Some projects may fail and other projects may slip, but that doesn't mean that the culture isn't committed or that individuals should be punished. Leaders know how to differentiate occasional failures from failures that are the result of commitments not taken seriously.

A promise to deliver is a promise that should be kept. You can make three mistakes here. The first is to commit to something you can't deliver, the second is to not take your own commitment seriously, and the third is to avoid making a commitment because you are afraid of failure. You must treat anything you promise as a serious matter that others are counting on. Let others know that a commitment you have made is important to you by measuring yourself against the commitment and making this measurement public.

To avoid the first mistake—making commitments you can't deliver—you must carefully review the prior performance of the team and strike a balance with your own personal experiences. Leaders should make sure they understand what they are committing to and how they will deliver it successfully. Also understand that, as a leader, you must deliver on your commitment consistently; and you need to know that one miss can quickly erode all the earlier successes.

Meeting commitments establishes trust between a leader and her team, and establishing team trust is vital. To establish trust, leaders must: (1) be consistent with the messages they give to everyone; (2) not take someone else's good ideas and sell them as their own; (3) not turn on their own team in public; (4) never put their team members in awkward positions, even when they may have made a mistake; (5) privately guide their team so they don't make mistakes again; (6) always be available to support their team and to talk to team members; (7) not rely on their authority alone to make things happen, but work actively to earn their team members' respect; (8) delegate tasks and intervene only when absolutely necessary (9) not compete with their own team members and (10) keep their word.

> *Flashback: Introducing Mr. Can't Estimate, a brilliant engineer who had answers for any technical question except for estimating time for completing tasks. He froze every time anyone asked him, How long will it take to do this? He would not respond or would say "two weeks" for everything. Most of his managers took the two-week answers but were very surprised more often than not. He would finish some tasks in a day and some other tasks in eight weeks. Eventually, Mr. Can't Estimate was only put on tasks that were not time critical and long term projects. In general, engineers underestimate the time it takes to do things. So as a manager you need to gauge your direct reports on their estimations and add some margin appropriately. If you have a new direct report, then add a bigger margin until you gain more knowledge about his or her abilities.*

Leaders should also work to create a sense of belonging and connection in the organization. Once something has happened to break trust, the leader will become irrelevant to the team, which will inevitably lead to a loss of top talent. A good leader knows that while trust is built slowly over years, it can be lost in a few seconds.

Teaching the team to honor commitment can be a powerful corporate tool to mature the organization and achieve excellence in execution. All leaders, vice presidents, directors, and managers must honor their commitments consistently. Occasional inconsistencies and/or missed commitments must be taken seriously by leaders, and the reasons for these failures must be communicated openly to the organization as a whole.

Honoring commitments goes beyond promising dates and numbers. It also includes information integrity. A commitment to deliver data or information must always be provided with honesty and high integrity. Departments such as marketing, engineering, or operations must commit to design, build, market, and deliver the product with every ounce of the accuracy and integrity to which they originally committed themselves.

It's true that sometimes, due to unforeseeable events, it's impossible to meet certain commitments—that's to be expected. But the team that respects commitments will always step up when needed by engaging their best people and working hard to achieve what they set out to do to the absolute best of their abilities.

Committing is not just about meeting dates and making money. It's about the culture you create and how you personally practice all elements of leadership, both professionally and in your personal life, thereby setting an exemplary standard for all.

CHAPTER 11

# Conclusion

This book is intended to help technical managers become leaders and to help businesses increase productivity and profitability. In this book, a manager is defined as a person who has direct reports regardless of their level or title in the organization. Most corporations spend tremendous amounts of time and money discussing how to improve results. My belief is that this will happen naturally—as long as the company matures leaders top to bottom and focuses on middle management. Individual contributors can work to their maximum ability, but properly harnessing this energy depends on the effectiveness of the organization's leaders.

Many corporations conduct management training classes. However, training classes are useless unless management *at all levels* practices the skills being taught. Leaders must walk the talk and coach their subordinates if they want to help them grow and improve. Taking management classes for a few hours once a year is not sufficient to train people to be good leaders.

Typically, the only tangible result of these training classes is to allow the HR department or top management to check off a box on their responsibility list.

All too often, the top executives implement management training to absolve themselves from spending their own time training or coaching. In doing so, executives throw away the opportunity to create close bonds with their direct reports. They also inadvertently devalue the training classes because they don't appear personally committed to the program.

Managers mistakenly think they don't have the time to train others and that therefore it's okay to ignore growing the capability of the team. The brutal reality is that understanding the importance of coaching middle management is a key factor in the overall success of the corporation. It is every manager's job *at every level* to train and coach their people. Good leadership should be contagious throughout the organization.

The ten chapters of this book capture the values managers should possess and the behaviors they need to demonstrate in order to succeed as mature and professional leaders. A company with strong leaders at all levels has an excellent chance for long-term success in the marketplace. While it may seem intuitive to draw that conclusion, most corporations fail to fully understand the importance of the behavior of every manager in their organization.

My final piece of advice is to study and learn from other successful leaders. In addition to all the values of good leadership outlined in this book, I've learned that great leaders generally share the following six attitudes and philosophies about life.

First, they are optimistic. They are pure optimism from head to toe and they always see the world in a positive light. Their optimism gives them a clear and positive self image, which they project into a bright and upbeat future. While remaining optimistic, they expect great things to happen to them. And, usually, they do!

Second, great leaders always look for the "double win." They are not selfish, and when they win, they like all the stakeholders of the company to win as well. Of course this means they want their competition to lose, but only in a fair game. Leaders look for the good in others and constantly create other winners to share in their success.

Third, leaders are passionate about everything they do in life. They know how to make every day count. Effective leaders know that each day should be like an Olympic gold medal day—there is no turning the clock backwards, no "redo" button in life. Consequently, they plan carefully, always looking forward and never dwelling on the past. Their motto is: "Learn from the past, live in the present, and be the architect of a beautiful future."

Fourth, great leaders make self-discipline and learning an ongoing concern. They read books, observe other good leaders' methods, and continually expand their knowledge. Self-discipline must become a habit and a natural way of doing things, and leaders make sure that it is.

Fifth, the best leaders surround themselves with good people. They know how to stay away from negative people and reject demotivating talk.

Sixth and finally, leaders strive to stay mentally and physically healthy. They know that the human body is a magnificent machine that nourishes their brain, so they take good care of it, pushing it to achieve great and wonderful things.

**Summary of leadership values:**

1. **Leaders inspire and energize the organization.**
2. **Leaders surface and face the "brutal reality."**
3. **Leaders communicate, communicate, and communicate some more.**
4. **Leaders look for the greater good of the company.**
5. **Leaders promote improvements relentlessly.**
6. **Leaders follow through on everything.**
7. **Leaders reward people fairly and consistently.**
8. **Leaders understand that the right people are their best assets.**
9. **Leaders commit to stretch goals.**
10. **Leaders value commitment.**

I hope this book has inspired you to be the greatest leader you can be. Here's to your future success.

# References

1. James C. Collins, *Good to Great: Why Some Companies Make the Leap ... and Others Don't* (New York : HarperCollins, 2001)
2. James C. Collins and Jerry I. Porras, *Built To Last: Successful Habits of Visionary Companies* (New York : Harper Business, 1997)
3. Jack Welch, Suzy Welch, *WINNING* (New York, Harper Business 2005)
4. Richard A. D'Aveni with Robert Gunther, *Hypercompetition: Managing the Dynamics of Strategic Maneuvering* (New York, The Free Press, 1994)
5. Larry Bossidy and Ram Charan, *EXECUTION: The Discipline Of Getting Things Done* (New York, Crown business, 2002)

# About the Author

Engineer and technology executive Ara W. Nazarian brings three decades of real-world experience to this book. A respected member of the technology industry with twenty United States-issued patents, the author earned his BSEE and MSEE from California State University, Los Angeles. Nazarian brings a wide spectrum of leadership expertise through many years of work both at several start-ups and large, multinational corporations, such as Broadcom and Western Digital.

CPSIA information can be obtained at www.ICGtesting.com
Printed in the USA
LVOW080133300112

266144LV00001B/36/P